Disclaimer: The author makes no guarantees concerning the level of success you may experience by following the advice and strategies contained in this book. The information is designed to present the author's opinion about the subject matter. The author obtained the information contained in this book from personal experience, education, and sources she believes to be reliable, but neither implies nor intends any guarantee of accuracy. The author believes that the information presented is sound, but readers are counseled to seek independent legal, accounting, and professional advice if required. The author particularly disclaims any liability loss, or risks taken by individuals acting directly or indirectly on the information contained herein.

Dedication

For Monica Weseman Carpenter, my friend, mentor and professor. Gone too soon.
Thank you for always believing in me.

For Dr. Dana Tesone, who believed in the places I would go.

For my parents, Conrad and Hilda Smith. Love you always and forever.

Table of Contents

Introduction

Thank you for purchasing this book. Follow the steps that I outline and by the end of this book you will know how to successfully start, grow, and scale one or more businesses in the Caribbean. I will help you to identify the cultural, social, and emotional fears that have held you back, and show you how to overcome them.

This book will give you guidance for mastering an entrepreneurial mindset, self-assessments for eliminating the limiting beliefs you may hold, such as risk aversion, perceived lack of support (crabs in a barrel), the fear of ownership, and the tools for replacing your limiting beliefs with empowering beliefs.

You will learn how to assess the skills you already have, use them to determine the ideal first business to start quickly with a limited budget, and how to use your unique story to market and attract your dream clients to your business.

Grab a notebook, and get ready to push past your fears, get off the sidelines, and create your successful business in the Caribbean. Whether you're trying to start a side business to supplement your income, or replace your income by growing a full-time business, you can do it, and I can show you how. Let's get started.

Steps to Starting Your Business

- Master your mindset.
- Develop your skillset.
- Eliminate limiting beliefs.
- Find your passion (Using the S.A.U.C.E. formula).
- Research your market. Who else is doing what you're doing (competition) and what do they charge (pricing).
- Identify trade or membership associations related to the business you want to start and decide if becoming a member will accelerate your business objectives based on the cost of joining.
- Test your idea. Find people willing to try your service or recipe at a discounted price in exchange for honest feedback.
- Find resources. Identify business grants or other resources that you can get to minimize your startup costs. Google, Amazon, and the library are some places where you can search for information. Know how much money you will need to start.
- Fund your business. Consider starting a skill or service-based business that provides time and convenience (and may have a lower startup cost), as opposed to a product-based business which may require inventory and have higher startup costs.
- If operating a food-based business, apply for any necessary food handling licenses.
- If the facility where the food will be prepared needs to be inspected, apply for inspection with the appropriate agency.
- For service or product-based businesses, apply for any required business or trade licenses.
- For skill-based businesses, such as plumber or electrician, present proof of certification at the time of the licensing application, if required.
- For retail product-based businesses, find out if there are any tax exemptions when importing goods for resale.
- Determine your delivery method. How will potential clients find you? Will you have a physical store or office? Do you plan on using technology such as an email or website to attract and contact clients? Can you manufacture your products in your home and deliver them to your clients?

- Determine your pricing, and your pricing structure. Create a manual or electronic system for tracking revenue and expenses. Depending on your budget, it could be as simple as a numbered receipt book and ledger book for manual tracking, or an expense tracking software.
- Once the business starts generating revenue and growing, you may decide to hire a bookkeeper and/or accountant to handle the tracking of your revenue and expenses. Even when you reach that stage, you need to understand the process and the numbers, to maintain maximum control of your business.
- Start the business. Write or find someone to write a series of press releases to announce that you're starting your business, another once you have started your business, and as often as necessary to announce significant business milestones.
- Know your exit strategy. How long do you plan on running the business? When you no longer want to be involved in the daily operation, will you hire employees to continue to run it? Would you be open to selling the business if someone offered to buy it?
- Building your business with an exit strategy in mind allows you to make decisions that align with your goals, and affects the way you scale (grow) the business.
- You can use this free business template from the SCORE organization to help you plan out your business. You can also find the template here: https://s3.amazonaws.com/mentoring.redesign/s3fs-public/SCORE-Deluxe-Startup-Business-Plan-Template_1.docx

Considerations for Starting Your Business

- It may require special licensing (e.g. food handler license or trade/professional license).
- Can be started at home, but might require special space (e.g. a commercial kitchen) and/or special equipment to grow and scale the business.
- For food related businesses, must have the ability to preserve freshness of food and adequate temperatures for raw and cooked food; potential for spoilage and loss due to inaccurate estimates of consumption leading to waste. A back-up generator is also a must in order to endure periods of time without electricity.
- Knowledge of delivery and distribution channels; will your business be primarily face-to-face, online, and does it give you the ability to work alone and on a flexible schedule?
- Does the business depend on your presence to function, or can the process be automated to minimize the need for your constant involvement (i.e. trading one job for another job that you own).
- Once you start the business, you have to find ways of attracting clients to a business. Newspaper advertising, radio advertising, social media (Facebook, Instagram, Twitter, LinkedIn), volunteering in your community, doing radio and newspaper interviews, and sponsoring events and organizations in your community can generate visibility and positive word of mouth for your business.
- Potential for deviant customers to negatively affect the reputation of your business with negative reviews or word of mouth. Having an established and effective service recovery model, or the process through which customer complaints and inquiries are handled, is key to minimizing this occurrence.

Exercise: Protecting Your Business Reputation

Do any of these considerations apply to your business? What are some ways that you think you can protect your business reputation?

Protecting Your Business Reputation

Finding Your Dream Client

When starting a new business, sometimes it's tempting to try to attract as many clients as you can in hopes that you will find enough people willing to pay for what you're selling. The problem with that is, if you don't know who your ideal client is, you will waste a lot of effort, time, and money marketing to people who don't need, don't want, or are unwilling to pay the price for your products or services. The more specific you are, the more likely you are to find the right clients. With that in mind, here are some considerations for attracting your ideal client:

- Who are they?
- What age group and generation do they belong to?
- What is their income?
- Do they have to make a certain amount of money to afford what I'm selling?
- Are they single or married?
- Do they have children?
- What do they like to do?
- What are their hobbies?
- What's important to them?
- Are they already paying for what I offer?
- Am I introducing a new product or service to my market?
- How am I educating my ideal client on who I am and what I offer? How can I express that I'm the right person to help them?
- Will I expect them to be a repeat customer?
- What value will I provide to ensure that they are?
- What is their need or problem?
- How am I solving it for them?
- What value am I delivering to make them see me as better and different than my competition?
- Where do I find my dream client? What industries are they in?
- What media do they engage with? Do they read the newspaper? Listen to the radio? Are they on social media?
- Are they already spending money on the services I offer (who is my competition)?

- Where am I serving them (do they come to me or do I go to where they are)? When are they most likely to need my product or service?
- Is it a one-time purchase or a repeat buy?
- Can I set them up on a schedule to provide them with my product or service automatically?
- How are my clients finding me?
- Do I plan to find my dream clients by paying for advertising, word of mouth, or from other client referrals?
- Are there other products that I can sell them based on the excellent service I give them?

The more specific and honest you are in describing their attributes, the better. Remember, you are describing your perfect client, who is willing to pay premium price for your product or service.

<u>Exercise: A Day with my Dream Client</u>

Review the information presented on identifying your dream client. Use as many of the questions above to describe your dream client and what a day with them would look and feel like. In this scenario, they can afford to and are willing to pay you whatever you ask, provided that you can articulate that you're the right person to help them. Feel free to put you desired income goal from the client if you have a number in mind. Describe a day with your dream client below;

A Day With My Dream Client

Mastering Your Entrepreneurial Mindset

- Push past your fear, and avoid analysis by paralysis. It's better to try and fail, than to continue to sit on the sidelines stifling your greatness doing nothing.
- Embrace your fear to conquer it. Make a list of the worst that could happen. Then make a list of what's the best that could happen. Then choose to change.
- Be grateful for everything.
- Make people feel valued and appreciated.
- Find a mentor that is already doing what you want to do successfully and ask them to guide you. The right mentor will help you in setting and achieving your goals and will hold you accountable and within deadlines.
- Don't be scared of the word "no". Turn the no into a maybe, the maybe into a wait, and the wait into a yes. Be patient and determined.
- Consistency creates credibility. Customers should not have to dread doing business with you based on your moods.
- Commit to a life of service. You will give excellent service to people who might not appreciate it or recognize it. You have to be okay with that.
- Be authentic and honest. Integrity is your most important asset.
- When you make a commitment, honor it. Your reputation for integrity is not replaceable. Honesty is the only policy. It's also the best one. Be honest with yourself and others in all situations.
- Poverty begins and ends with your mindset.

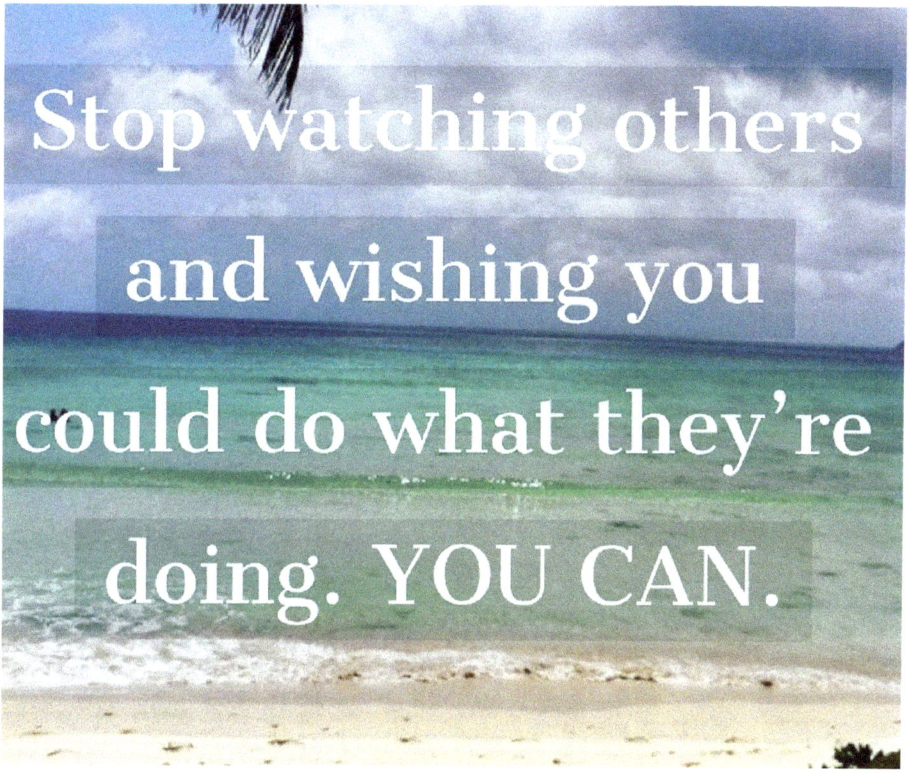
Stop watching others
and wishing you
could do what they're
doing. YOU CAN.

Developing Your Skillset

- To develop your skillset, you can expand on your existing education by figuring out what you want to learn, and finding the means to learn it for free or at a minimal cost.
- If there is a library in your community, that's a good place to start.
- On social media, you can find experts and influencers on various topics. You can search Facebook for groups that match your interests, Instagram for pages on topics relating to your interests and people who teach online and offer webinars and master classes.
- LinkedIn is a tool for networking, and you can find articles on a variety of business topics there.
- Udemy, Teachable, and Thinkific offer online courses that you can take at your own pace.
- Amazon offers a book subscription service called Kindle Unlimited that charges a monthly fee, but gives you the ability to borrow up to ten books at a time. There are literally thousands of books available to borrow that can be read on your computer, tablet, or phone using the Kindle application.
- Community colleges offer an alternative for learning new skills, because you can take individual courses without pursuing a degree.
- Technical colleges are another avenue for learning skills such as electrician, plumber, and mechanic, among others.
- You also can try to get a job in a field that you eventually want to start a business in, and learn skills on-the-job, for example work as a baker or prep cook in a restaurant to learn how to cook on a commercial scale.
- You also can try find someone who is doing what you want to do as a business and ask them if they are willing to mentor you.

Exercise: What's Your Skillset?

Name some skill that you feel you already have. Next, name some skills you would like to learn. Is there anything stopping you from learning new skills?

What's Your Skillset?

Eliminating Your Limiting Beliefs

20 Examples of Limiting Beliefs

1. The "crabs in a barrel" will try to keep me down if I start a business.
2. Nobody is going to support my business.
3. I have a secure job. I don't want to give it up.
4. I'm not smart enough to run a business.
5. I don't have the time to start a business. I don't have enough money to start a business.
6. I'm scared of failing.
7. I don't want people to think I'm a failure.
8. There's nothing wrong with being poor.
9. This is the wrong time to start a business.
10. I have too much going on. I'm not starting a business to help these ungrateful people.
11. It's too risky to start a business.
12. I don't want people talking bad about me.
13. If I start a business, people will be jealous.
14. I'm too broke to start a business.
15. I'll start a business soon.
16. My family was poor and I turned out alright.
17. I don't have a place to start my business.
18. I don't have the ability to run a business.
19. I love my job and my job loves me.
20. There's no way I can start a business now.

Examples of Empowering Beliefs

- Procrastination is killing my dream of starting a business.
- I am stronger than my fear.
- There is nothing more important than building a better life for myself and my family and starting a business is the way I will do that.
- I am up to the challenge of starting a business.
- Failure is not an option because too many people are depending on me to succeed. I will start and I will keep going, even if it seems rough.
- Change is uncomfortable, but I'm up to the challenge.
- My goals are bigger than my fears.
- I can't keep waiting for tomorrow to start.
- Tomorrow never comes. I am stronger than I think, and braver than I give myself credit for.
- Failure is not fatal.
- I have planned for success and if I fail, I can start again.
- Poverty begins and ends with my mindset.
- I have the power to change my circumstances.
- I can do the same thing I do for my job for myself and benefit.
- I know what I want and I can ask for it.
- There are opportunities available to me everywhere.
- I'm willing to learn and grow as necessary to run a successful business.
- I have the ability to evaluate and change my circumstances.
- I see the good in situations and maintain a positive mindset.
- I think before I speak, and I don't deliberately slander or hurt people.
- I conduct myself with honesty and integrity at all times.
- I am grateful for everything that has brought me to this point in my life.
- I choose to succeed, not struggle.
- "Broke" is temporary; "Broken" is permanent.
- I am committed to being successful in everything that I do.
- I am breaking the generational curse of poverty in my family.
- I can start a business by myself or with my family.

- I am smart, I am confident, and I have the skills and ability to reach any level of success that I desire.
- I deserve to be successful.
- I am kind to myself and others.
- I share my knowledge and I give back to my community.

It all starts with why. Once you figure out your why, you can make your why happen. Why do you want to start a business; what is your motivation for doing so? Knowing your why helps you to figure out what you love, what you're good at, and what your purpose is. Once you understand your purpose, you can monetize your gift.

<u>Exercise: Create Your Own Empowering Beliefs</u>

Write down as many empowering beliefs as you can think of below, based on the successful life that you are trying to create. Refer to them often and commit them to memory. They will form the foundation for the successful, profitable business that you are about to start.

<u>Exercise: Eliminating Your Limiting Beliefs</u>

Review the examples of limiting beliefs, and the examples of empowering beliefs. For each limiting beliefs you know you have, find a corresponding empowering belief to replace it with. Write your empowering beliefs below. Create affirmations from the empowering beliefs that you chose to replace for your limiting beliefs. Feel free to create your own empowering affirmations. Repeat your new empowering affirmations to yourself daily.

Creating Your Own Empowering Beliefs

Eliminating Your Limiting Beliefs

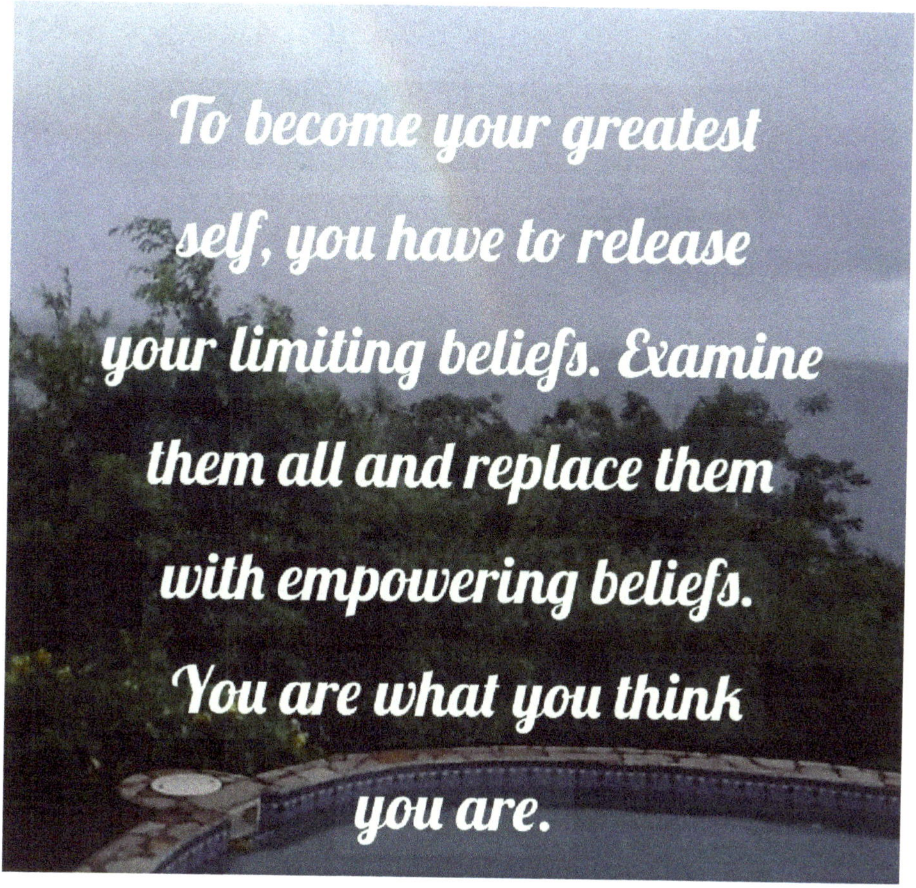
To become your greatest
self, you have to release
your limiting beliefs. Examine
them all and replace them
with empowering beliefs.
You are what you think
you are.

Things I Wish I Knew Sooner

- You are what you think you are.
- Find what you love and do that.
- Live a life of service.
- It all starts with why.
- Money is leverage. Money is freedom.
- Fear is not fatal.
- It's natural to be scared. Do it anyway.
- Starting is the hardest step.
- Inspire others by your actions; inspire yourself by maintaining your perseverance and determination. If you like it, make it a hobby. If you love it, make it a business.
- Don't be scared to try new hobbies. Think of it as market research.
- To progress, you must own your unique core story and identify in yourself what makes you special, different, and better.
- Make a list of the challenges that you have overcome, and recognize that you are unstoppable and resilient.
- Start a business. Start small. Start it on the side, but start. It's time to benefit from your skills and hard work.
- Stop raising employees and start raising entrepreneurs. Start a family business and lead by example.
- Your million dollar idea is being held hostage by your one dollar mindset. It's time to plan it, execute it, and release it!
- Commit to being bold, making a plan, and launching a business doing something you love.
- Confidence is the bridge that separates the thinkers from the doers. Stop waiting for someone else to be your #1 fan.
- Make today the day that you decide what you want. Then plan and dare to make it happen.
- Tomorrow doesn't exist. The best "boss" you'll ever have is you.
- Make it happen. Be positive, humble, and open to learning. The right people will come into your life and help you to level up.
- Tell yourself that "I am a procrastinator" is no longer an acceptable excuse. It's time to work. New decade, new greatness.
- The only way to find out if you will fall or fly is to leap. Starting is the hardest part, but it must be done.

- Ask for what you want. It's hard to achieve your goals when you're afraid to make your intentions known.
- Create a sustainable business by solving a problem or creating convenience.
- Create a business by finding a service gap and filling it. Stop telling yourself the lie that you can't run a business.
- If you can do it for a job, you can do it for yourself.
- Constantly invest in your development.
- If you like it, learn it.
- If you love it, live it.
- Move into the new decade with a clear mindset to be the greatest version of yourself possible.
- Believe that there is only greatness ahead of you.
- Dream like a child, but execute like an adult. It's time to exceed your goals.
- Be so exceptional at what you do that your critics will become your loyal clients.
- Give the excellent service that you expect as a customer.
- Desire, passion, and motivation can help you to define your gift.
- The earlier you define your gift, the easier it is to realize its full potential.
- Your gift should be something you're both good at and enjoy.
- Move toward what moves you.
- Your goals should be fueled by desire.
- Start with the end goal in mind.
- You have to love what you're doing to make it sustainable.
- Your desire to achieve a goal should be stronger than the obstacles you will face or it's not worth pursuing.

Exercise: Letter to Your Past Self

Write a letter to younger self. Base it on the advice you wish you had then, knowledge and experiences that you have had up to now, and where you wish you were in life that you are not. What would your letter say? After you write it, go back and read your letter. It is the blueprint for changing your circumstances. You can't relive the past, but you can control your present, and plan your future to create the life that you want.

Letter to Your Past Self

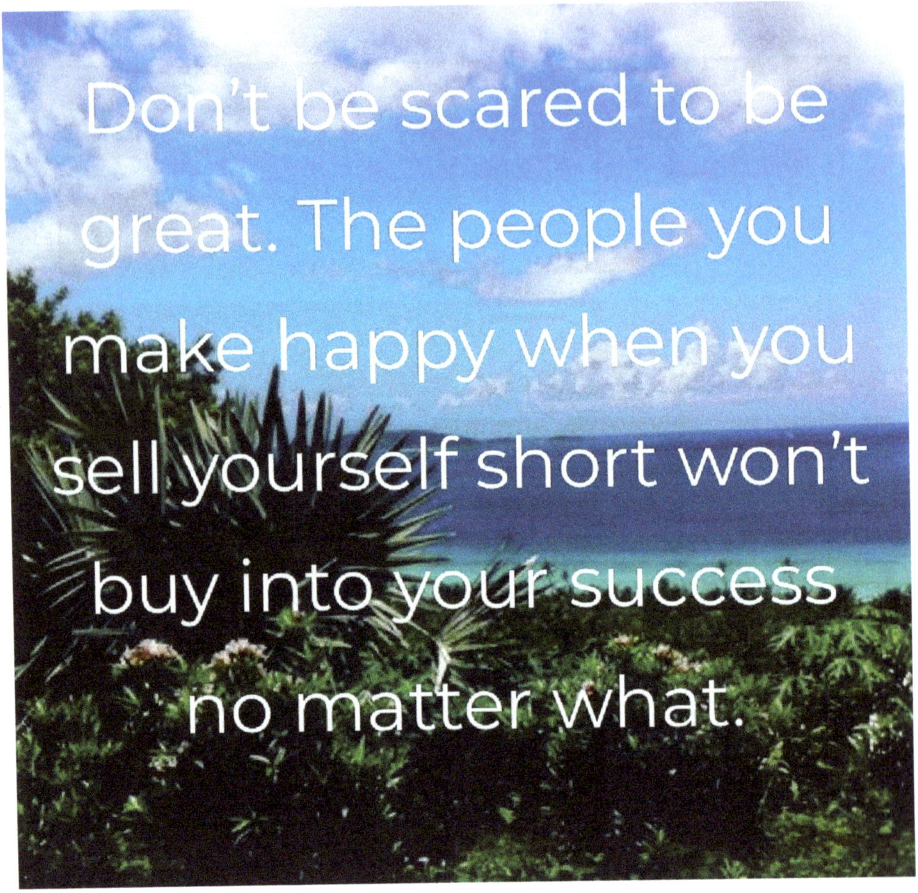
Don't be scared to be
great. The people you
make happy when you
sell yourself short won't
buy into your success
no matter what.

Specialist or Generalist: Understanding the Difference

Specialist

- Focus on one niche or specialty.
- Easier to describe what you do.
- Suitable if you already have a local reputation for being the best in a particular field. i.e. jewelry maker, chef, locksmith.
- Enough demand must exist in the specialization to scale into a full-time business.

Generalist

- Offer a combination of products or services.
- Harder to explain what your main business is to your client.
- Suitable for someone with complimentary skill sets (i.e., a notary public that is a photographer creates a package that marries people and provides photographs of the event).
- Suitable as a side hustle or to create multiple streams of income. Can be scaled into a full-time business.

It is easier for a specialist to position themselves as an expert. Being a specialist does not prevent you from pursuing multiple streams of income. The more tightly you can narrow your focus, the faster you can identify your dream client and begin doing business. Finding your passion is the way to do that, so it's time to discover your S.A.U.C.E.

Finding Your Passion: What's Your S.A.U.C.E.?

S: Skills and Style Service

Skills: Your skills are comprised of what you think you're good at, as well as what people tell you you're good at. Be honest with yourself. Are you good enough at it that people will pay you consistently to do it? If you're not good enough yet, is it something that you can continue to practice, develop, or learn until you're good enough? Make sure that you include things you love doing within your skillset, because those are the things you will be willing to master and consistently develop into a sustainable business.

Service Style: Within a job setting, do you like working alone or in a group? When starting a business, especially when you are the business, you need to be personable and approachable. You also need to be consistently excellent in the service you provide. Your service is your reputation. One thing you can do, however, is select a business that involves less client interaction, as opposed to more. An example of this is being a plumber versus being a singer, or being a house cleaner versus being a store owner. The expected levels of customer interaction are less for certain types of businesses.

A: Attitudes and Advantages

Attitudes: In the context of deciding the business you want to start, attitudes relate to the way that you perceive clients, and to the way that you are perceived in the community you want to start a business in. If you love interacting with people, a high contact (service) business is ideal, whereas if you think of customers as a revenue stream but don't particularly like interacting, a skill-based business might be more suitable. In both case, it helps to have a community reputation for being professional, efficient, and approachable prior to starting your business.

Advantages: These are assets or skills that you possess prior to starting the business that will make it easier for you to start, grow, and scale a successful business. Examples of this are: a unique product that you created, knowledge of a recipe for a food or dessert that is highly in demand, an excellent reputation at your current job, to the extent that when you start a business those customers will become your loyal followers.

U: Unique Story and Selling Proposition

Unique Story: Knowing your "why" for starting your business is crucial to your unique story. Your memorable experiences, challenges that you have overcome, family relationships, reasons for starting the business, and how you want to help your community by starting your business all form your unique story. Develop a 30 second summary (elevator pitch) that encompasses those elements that you can use to tell your unique story.

Unique Selling Proposition (a.k.a. The Elevator Pitch: Chances are that unless you are creating a product or service that didn't exist before to start your business (which is unlikely, but not impossible), you need to be able to explain and articulate to your clients why they should choose to support your business. Quality, convenience, superior service, and differentiation from your competitors can form the basis for your unique selling proposition. I don't recommend incorporating price into your USP. You have to believe that you are worth a premium price and charge accordingly. Otherwise you're just going from a job you work for to a job you own.

C: Credentials and Credibility

Credentials: Your credentials are your signature. They are the reason that people will know that you are who you say you are and can deliver excellently and consistently on the products or services you provide. Your credentials consist of your achievements, commendations, awards, special training, and any elements in your unique story that make you different and better at your chosen business or profession.

Credibility: Your credibility is your authenticity. Your honesty and integrity form a part of your credibility. Your reputation for delivering on time and as promised, your transparency and fairness in your service delivery and pricing, and the goodwill that you have built within and throughout your community by volunteering, mentoring, and delivering service above and beyond what is expected all contribute to your credibility.

E: Education and Entrepreneurial Strengths

Education: This is any formal knowledge that you have acquired in a structured setting to improve or acquire the skillset for the business you are providing. Education can include a high school diploma and college education, but can also consist of less traditional settings, such as vocational schools, apprenticeships, internships, military training or certifications.

Entrepreneurial Strengths: Your entrepreneurial strengths consist of the areas of your business that you feel proficient in handling. It's different functions necessary to run your business and determine whether you are proficient or not. Some examples are billing, marketing, accounting, and hiring. You can then choose to study to improve those specific skills or outsource those functions if you can afford to. Doing so frees you to leverage your time in the most efficient way to maximize profitability.

Exercise: Discover Your S.A.U.C.E.

Your sauce is unique to you. Take the time to complete this assessment. This exercise will give you the foundation to identifying the ideal business to start. You can do this exercise multiple times and change it as your business grows. Once you have completed the assessment, combine and eliminate elements until you reach the ideal mix of what you want to incorporate into your business.

Discovering Your S.A.U.C.E.

Skills I have:

My service style is:

My business attitude is:

My **advantages** are:

My unique story is:

My **unique selling proposition** is:

My **credentials** are:

My credibility comes from:

My education is:

My **entrepreneurial strengths** are:

Pricing Your Services

There are many factors that you can use to determine your pricing and the payment methods you will accept:

- **How will you get paid?**
- **Will your business primarily accept cash?**
- **Will your business only accept cash?**
    - If so, you need to find a way to protect yourself and your funds, either with a safe or by making regular bank deposits and tying your cash to a business debit card.
- **Will you accept credit cards?**
    - If so, you will need to set up a merchant account at your bank and make sure you understand the fees for both the equipment to run the payments and the transaction fees. You will need to factor these fees into your pricing to pass that cost onto your clients.
- **How will you bill your clients if you're providing professional services?**
    - You need to know how to invoice and bill for your services. Make sure that all the terms, conditions, and if applicable, guarantees are clearly explained in the contract or invoice. If necessary, consult an attorney on drafting a template contract.
    - I recommend that you collect a partial deposit before starting any work, at least 50 percent of the total fee, plus your expenses. Agree on a completion date for the service or project, and state in the invoice that the remaining balance is due upon completion of the work. Clearly articulate that any work or service will not be completed or delivered until payment in full is received.
    - Decide on a cancellation fee and clearly state in the invoice or contract the dollar amount or percentage of the total fee that you will keep if the client cancels the work. That prevents you from working without getting compensation.
    - Understand that you are bringing massive value to every client and that you deserve to charge a premium price for what you're offering. Think of a price that frightens you, or what you would be willing to pay if you were the client, then double it (or if you're feeling bold triple it).

<u>Exercise: Your Payment System</u>

Consider the factors above and answer the questions as they relate to the business you want to start.

Your Payment System

But What Do I Charge?

There are many factors in deciding what to charge:

- Is your business a full-time venture or a side hustle?
- How much money to you want to net in profit after all expenses and overhead are paid out?
- Will you be paying yourself a salary from the business, or are you re-investing the profits back into the business?
- How many hours per day or per week will you be devoting to working at and growing your business?
- Do you have competitors offering the same service? What are they charging?
- Are you the sole owner, or are there partners and investors that will need to be paid distributions from the business profits?
- Will you have employees, and if so, what benefits will you be offering them?

Pricing For Service-Based Businesses:

Determine all the costs associated with providing your service; equipment, licensing, certifications, memberships, advertising and promotional items, uniforms, transportation costs, etc.
Is your service saving the client time, money, or both?

Example: You can decide how much you want to earn and figure out the best pricing structure to help you meet your goal. For example, to make $100,000 in one year, you can complete projects for five clients billing $20,000 per project, or you could get four clients paying you a $10,000 dollar per month retainer, and complete three projects billing $20,000 per project.

You could also base your pricing on what your competitors charge for the same services you provide, but remember that if you don't charge enough or are scared to price yourself according to your worth and the value you bring to the table, you will get frustrated. You don't want to trade a job you work for, only to get into a job you own because you're not charging enough. **Your goal should be financial freedom without trading your hours for dollars.**

In any event, you need to be able to present and explain to your client how your service will save them significantly more than the fee that they are paying you. Educate yourself on systems and applications that can automate some, if not most, of the work you will need to do to make your business profitable and successful. As we progress, I will show you how to do that.

Exercise: Determine Your Price

Thinking of the business you plan to start, what pricing structure will you be using? How much do you want to earn? How will you communicate your value to your dream client? Are you saving them time, money, both, or something else?

Determine Your Price

A Story About Trust

As a child when I was growing up in the British Virgin Islands, I used to hear the expression "Let me trust this until I get paid" or "I need you to trust me until I can pay you." I never understood until I got older that because of the close knit nature and relationships, it was a cultural thing that some customers felt comfortable enough to ask the shop owners to "trust" them by giving them the goods without receiving payment. With the implied promise that when the customer got the money they would return and pay for the goods.

When I lived back home in the 1990's, I started an event planning and advertising company that also sold promotional items. Because I did not know then what I know now, I ordered promotional items such as pens and mugs for my clients and only required a 50 percent deposit to place the order with the "trust" that I would be paid the rest when the items arrived and were delivered to the client.

Another Caribbean slang I learned about is called "bad pay." I found out the hard way that by not collecting the payment in full, and because the items were branded with the company names of the clients, I was either stuck with items that were of no use to me and I could not re-sell, or I could release the items to the clients and "trust" them to pay me. Usually I delivered the items and relied on "trust."

After numerous attempts to collect my money, I realized that I had made the mistake of selling to people that were "bad pay" and had no intention of ever paying me in full for my goods and services.

I made that mistake because I knew, liked, and trusted the people, and because they were prominent business owners in the community. I never thought that they were dishonest and had no intention of paying in full. Over 20 years later, the same people still owe me money, and it is dead debt that is non-collectable.

I made many mistakes and learned many valuable lessons from that experience. I learned that I was pricing my products way too low, since the catalogs came from the United States with the prices printed in the catalogs. Once clients saw the prices in the catalogs, they would question the markup on prices, even though they knew that there were extra costs associated with getting the products shipped to the Caribbean. If I had to do it over, I would re-label the catalogs showing my prices, or show them a picture of the item and quote them my price.

Another thing I learned is that you have to have written invoices and receipts for every transaction, to be able to track who owes you, how much they owe you, and when the payments are due.

The next thing I learned is to collect payment in full in advance for products. Services have a lower overhead since they are based on your knowledge and effort, so you can be more flexible on billing.

Products have fixed costs that you need to collect upfront for, plus you need to at least double or triple the price in order to profit because of the higher shipping, import, and added costs of getting goods to the Caribbean. If you're going to be scared to markup your products, selling products is not the right business for you and you will not last in business.

Another thing I learned from my time as a business owner was that you have to be consistent in dealing with clients. Getting into the habit of lowering your prices, giving discounts and selling on trust will destroy your business. Once clients know that you don't have enough belief in your product or service to sell it confidently, unapologetically, and to make the profit you want to, some clients will try to take advantage of you and call it "trying to get a deal."

My final takeaway was that every client is not your dream client. You have to be strong enough and willing to turn down business from bad clients in order for your business to survive and thrive.

My previous business ownership experience is why I am a believer that you have to master an entrepreneurial mindset before you start your business. I was so happy to have clients, that I was willing to settle for less and as a result was taken advantage of.

You have to be comfortable with money. Get used to talking about money, asking for money, getting paid richly for what you do or sell, and becoming successful and wealthy. Otherwise you will have an employee mindset in a business that you own. Profiting from owning your business is not greedy, it's necessary.

Exercise: Beliefs About Money

Can you think of any cultural beliefs, slangs, or habits that you were taught about money and business ownership when you were growing up?

Beliefs About Money

Pathways to Entrepreneurship

Convenience Entrepreneurship

Convenience-Based Business Examples:

Grocery and personal shopper for a client-- this involves consulting with the client on their needs and learning their personal preferences. You add value by acting as a concierge/personal valet who learns their habits and preferences, and not only shops but delivers and organizes the purchased items in a way that is easy for the client to access and keep track of.

A hair stylist that braids hair and offers natural hair care solutions. Using their expertise, they offer style and product recommendations to the client, in addition to the braiding and styling of the hair. The stylist can add value by establishing a schedule with the client, as well as sourcing the products and selling them to the client, either at a profit or as part of a haircare package.

Food Entrepreneurship

Food Based Business Examples:

Baking: Full scale bakery, wholesale desserts to existing businesses, sell desserts at various businesses, sell desserts at functions and events, such as fairs and concerts.

Restaurant: Food truck, specialty food that can be sold wholesale or retail; recipes that are potentially suitable for export (i.e., specialty sauce, liqueur, or candy).

Catering: Private events at client's location, local cuisine, experience-based catering that incorporates a cooking demonstration as part of an authentic cultural experience.

Retail Sales: If you have a unique recipe, such as a hot pepper sauce, local drinks such as passion fruit juice or sorrel, or dessert such as tarts, cakes, or candies, consider producing it in batches and contracting with established vendors to sell in their retail stores. Re-invest the profits into production, with the goal of getting access to a commercial kitchen to be able to scale and grow the business.

Cultural Entrepreneurship

Cultural Business Examples:

Historian: Find people who know the history and have lived through different time periods of the development of the place where you live. Interview them and record their experiences, both in written and audio recordings. Turn the interview material into a book or audiobook.

Artist: If you have drawing, painting, or sculpting ability, create artwork based on things that are culturally unique to your island. It could be flowers, scenery, portraits, or anything that is readily identifiable with your destination.

Photographer: Take photographs of events such as carnivals or festivals and sell the images to media outlets, or on stock photography sites such as Shutterstock, Shutterfly, Getty Images, or iStock.

Musician: Play or learn to play a musical instrument and play in a band that represents the musical genre of your destination. I.e., steel pan, calypso, soca, or reggae.

Destination Entrepreneurship

Destination Business Examples:

Create and market tour packages centered on the local attractions of your destination. Establish your reputation as a local expert by researching the history of the places you'll be taking clients to tour.

Establish your credibility and visibility by blogging or writing articles about interesting places that you have discovered. Don't limit yourself to marketing just to tourists. Market your tours to locals who might want to learn more about your finds or have friends and family visiting that they want to take of tours.

Consider partnering with hotel operators and have them refer clients to you in exchange for a pre-determined percentage. Factor that cost into what you charge. Identify travel trade shows that you can attend to promote your tour business, and inquire to your local tourism board if they would be willing to split the cost of travel and attendance in exchange for you working at their booth and sharing your knowledge of the destination.

Sports Entrepreneurship

Sports entrepreneurship offers the aspiring entrepreneur the opportunity to leverage free resources such as the sun, sand, and especially the sea into a viable business. Activities such as swimming, snorkeling, volleyball that can be conducted on the beach with limited equipment that offers the opportunity to either conduct tours, create tournaments, or to teach for a fee (i.e., offer swimming lessons or conduct snorkeling tours.)

Another opportunity in sports entrepreneurship exists in creating tournaments and events. In this scenario, you could identify a location such as a basketball court, hiking trail, or beach, and create an event. Steps for doing this would involve calculating expenses, determining the desired profit that you want to generate from the event, creating attendance projections, and finding businesses to sponsor the event in exchange for advertising space on t-shirts.

Product Entrepreneurship

If you decide that you want to focus on selling a product or products, there are many ways that you can go about sourcing and selling products.

Note: In many cases, you will need to have a business license in order to be able to prove to manufacturers and wholesalers that you are a legitimate business entity that intends to re-sell. If you cannot establish your credibility, many vendors will be reluctant to offer you the lowest prices, or might even refuse to do business with you.

First, you have to decide what product or products you want to sell. Think of your business as the solution to a problem; what problem is your business going to solve?

For example, if you live in a place where it rains frequently, you could create a line of custom umbrellas and raincoats, branded with your company name. Or you could sell umbrellas that do not have your name or logo on them, but might promote tourism. The important thing is that people know that you sell high quality umbrellas that are wind resistant.

Notice that I did not talk about the price. When you focus on providing quality, exceptional service, and value, and the price becomes less of a factor in the buying decision, your clients will trust you. Your dream client is concerned with you solving their problem or pain point, and once you're doing that they will pay your price consistently and gladly. People will do business with you because they know you, like you, and/or trust you.

How do I Find the Products?

Once you decide what you want to sell, you have to be able to source the products, and buy them at a price that is comparable and competitive with what others who sell the same or similar products. The internet is a great resource for finding companies and their contact information.

Listed below are some manufacturer directories and manufacturer sources to get you started. Remember, some will require you to register and establish that you are a licensed business in order to establish accounts.

- https://www.thomasnet.com/ - This is a comprehensive directory of industries and manufacturers. You will need to register for a free account before you can access the information.
- https://www.alibaba.com/ - This is a directory of manufacturers from China.
- https://kaeser-blair.com/ - This is a company that offers the opportunity to start a promotional products business, but you can also use it to find your own products that you can re-sell.
- www.surfexpo.com - This is an excellent resource for finding and connecting with watersport equipment, resort equipment, apparel, and tourism related merchandise. This is a tradeshow that is held twice a year, usually in Orlando, Florida, usually in early September and early January. You will need a business license to register to attend the show.

As a new entrepreneur, you might not fully understand all the costs associated with getting your products to the Caribbean before you sell. Just because you have a license it doesn't mean you know what you're doing. Make sure that you are pricing correctly by factoring in all your expenses, and adding a healthy profit margin on your products. It is a good idea to work with a sales representative for each company that you are doing business with.

Exercise: List Your Products

Make a list of products that you currently use that you cannot find locally for purchase. Next, make a list of products that relate to skill or hobbies that you have. Compare the lists. Do you see any products on your list that solve a problem that you feel enough other people are having? For example, is it difficult to find party supplies? Restaurant supplies?

List Your Products

Drop shipping is a game-changer for entrepreneurs in the Caribbean, because selling online is not location dependent, and once you set up your store, the fulfilment of the orders is handled by the companies that you select for sourcing your dropship products. You are no longer limited to selling to people who are only where you are. You can market to anyone anywhere in the world.

In this scenario, you are responsible for marketing to your audience, getting customers to your site, for selecting and designing the logos and designs that will appear on the products you're selling and for pricing the products on your online store. You then order from the dropship supplier.

Make sure that you are pricing correctly by factoring in all your expenses, and adding a healthy profit margin on your products, at least double your cost plus expenses. Remember that the higher you price your item, the less amounts you have to sell to reach your desired income goal.

- https://www.oberlo.com- This is one option for finding products to sell in an online store. In this scenario, you find the clients, and Oberlo fulfills and ships the orders. You add your desired profit margin to the price that Oberlo is charging you and that is what you bill your buyer. You then order from Oberlo, and they pack, ship, and mail the item to your buyer. This is known as drop-shipping.
- https://www.shopify.com - This is a platform where you can build your online store. You can sell physical products, such as T-shirts, bags, mugs, etc. You also can create information products such as electronic books (eBooks), cookbooks, or instructional books to teach a skill you have and sell them on Shopify. You also can sell a combination of both.
- https://www.bigcommerce.com is another online shopping platform.
- https://www.printful.com - This site offers apparel and other items that can be printed on demand for your drop-shipping store. You would connect this account to your Shopify or BigCommerce site and when customers order your designs, printful would fulfill, pack and ship the order to your client.
- https://printify.com - This site is similar to printful.
- https://teespring.com - This is another alternative to printful and printify.

As you can see, there are many ways of finding products. You can use the internet and search for the product you want to sell. From our earlier umbrella example, you would do a google search for "wholesale umbrellas" or "umbrella manufacturers" or in our example, if you know that you want to especially sell Totes brand umbrellas, your search would be "Totes umbrellas" or "wholesale Totes umbrellas." The key is knowing what you want to sell, who your target client is going to be, and how many you have to sell at what price point to make the amount of money that you desire to make.

Service Entrepreneurship

Service entrepreneurship is ideal for starting a business in the Caribbean. There are many services that solve problems, save your clients money, provide convenience, or save your clients time. Service businesses often have low overhead and startup costs, which makes them ideal for both the person trying to supplement their current income, or transitioning into full-time entrepreneurship.

Here are some examples of low cost service businesses that you can start:

- If you love pets, you could start a dog walking and pet grooming business. You could supplement this income by selling pet toys and accessories. You can brand these items with your company name, which gives you free advertising that the client takes away with them.
- If you enjoy doing laundry, you could start a mobile laundry business. You would collect clothes that need to be cleaned from the client, wash, fold, and press (according to what the client requests) and deliver the clothes back to the client. You would add value by interviewing the client to make sure that they don't have any detergent allergies, and if they have any other preferences. You could either charge a fee per piece of clothing, or a set fee for the laundry service. Remember to factor all your costs (transportation, detergent, electricity, and the time that it takes you to clean and fold the clothes).
- If you speak more than one language, you could provide tutoring for children, teach an English for speakers of other languages course for adults, or provide document and live event translation services for businesses and business meetings. If you do decide to provide live translation services for businesses, that is a premium service, and you need to charge a higher fee. Research what live translators charge in your market. If that information is not available, get on the internet and research the price range that live translators charge. You have to be able to conduct yourself with honesty, integrity, and be accurate in what you're translating. Most importantly, you must maintain the confidentiality of the client.
- If you own a pickup truck, you could start a delivery service. You could deliver groceries, appliances, dirt, gravel, water, etc. You can charge per trip, per load, or based on what you're transporting and its value.

Exercise: List Your Potential Services

Based on your S.A.U.C.E, write a list of services that you can create a service business around.

List Your Potential Services

Skill Entrepreneurship

Skill based entrepreneurship can be created using a particular skill you have (i.e. electrician, plumber, mechanic, chef, etc.) or by teaching what you know, either in person or online.

Teaching online does not have to involve academic subjects. You can create a course on how to sew, how to cook Caribbean dishes, how to garden; basically about anything you can think of.

To create a business around a skill you have, you need to provide the service, plus promote your business, calculate your expenses, and bill your clients accordingly, so that you're not losing money. Remember to factor the cost of your education, occupational licenses, tools and materials into your pricing.

About Teaching Online

To teach online, you need to pick your topic, pick the platform that you're going to teach on, create the course, create a payment system, and create marketing so that clients can find you online when they search for the topic that you are teaching.

Another option if you are an expert in a subject is to create the learning content, then license the information to a company that can create the course. You would be paid a licensing fee for their right to produce and teach the course, plus a royalty fee every time they sell the course (per user or per class; this is a way of creating passive income, because you don't have to deal with students, creating the course, collecting payments, or customer service. You are being paid a percentage of the sales for your knowledge.

There are several teaching platforms that you can use to create and teach your course. You don't have to have the technical skills to build your course platform. There are freelance services such as www.fiverr.com/ and www.upwork.com where you can find someone who can build your course for you. You would only need to proofread the course beforehand to make sure that it represents your brand and the information that you are conveying in an accurate manner.

To get started, you can conduct a search online for different course platforms. Compare the pricing, the features, the support they provide in training you how to use their platform, and the customer service that they offer in setting up, maintaining, and using their platform. If you're just getting started or don't have much technical experience, contact a sales representative by phone or email.

Some online video teaching platforms include:

- www.udemy.com
- www.teachable.com
- www.thinkific.com
- www.kajabi.com
- www.zoom.com

About Ebooks

Another option if you don't want to create a video course is to create an electronic book (eBook), chart, drawing, or another digital product about a topic you want to teach, and then create a page to sell it from. You don't have to create a website, you can create one or several electronic books, decide on your pricing, and then upload them to a standalone site that will store your book. When someone orders your book and pays for it, an email with a link to the book is automatically sent to them. You make sure that connect your account is connected, to PayPal, Stripe, a bank account, or another payment portal. Your money, minus fees is deposited to your account, after a few days, or depending on the schedule that your payment portal specifies.

To get started, you can conduct a search online for different course platforms. Compare the pricing, the features, the support they provide in training you how to use their platform, and the customer service that they offer in setting up, maintaining, and using their platform. If you're just getting started or don't' have much technical experience, contact a sales representative by phone or email.

Some digital product delivery platforms include:

- www.kartra.com
- www.ontraport.com
- www.payhip.com
- www.bigcartel.com
- www.gumroad.com
- www.shopify.com

Entrepreneurship is the equalizer that can alleviate economic poverty. As a Caribbean citizen, you have the benefit of living daily in a place that tourists have to pay large sums of money to visit and enjoy. I firmly believe that there is no better time than now to assess where you are, determine where you want to be, and take the steps to make it happen.

The Caribbean islands each have their own personality, and although the information presented in this book can help people in other island economies and in places other than the Caribbean, my "why" for writing this book is to inspire the resilient, amazing, talented people of the Caribbean to start to believe in their greatness and to take the leap into entrepreneurship.

By learning to leverage the sun, sand, sea, and culture that is free to you but so valuable to tourists and others who pay handsomely to enjoy it, the citizens of the Caribbean can build profitable, scalable and successful businesses. It is my sincere hope that this book inspires you to take action.

Starting a business can change your life. Anyone can start a business. It doesn't matter whether you're a child with a great idea and supportive parents, a retiree looking for a way to transition into retirement and the next chapter of your life, a high school student that doesn't know whether to go to college or not, or a prisoner trying to reintegrate into society to make an honest living. Entrepreneurship can give you all that and more. It can give you economic stability, prosperity, and help you to create a legacy for you and your family.

Consistency, integrity, superior service, responsiveness, and service recovery will help you when things go wrong will take you far in your new business. It is my sincere hope that after reading this book, you have found enough ideas and inspiration to take the leap and get started.

Start. You're ready but you're not comfortable. Whatever you're afraid of doing, start. Mediocrity thrives in comfort.

Connect With Me

To connect with me, you can reach me on:

Facebook: Blanche Greaux

Twitter: @blanchegreaux

LinkedIn: Blanche Greaux

Instagram: @the_blanche_greaux

Email: blanchegreaux@gmail.com

You can also join the Profits from Paradise Facebook group. There, you can connect with a community of like-minded individuals venturing into Caribbean entrepreneurship. You can ask questions, share your progress and your fears, and share your victories as you progress on your entrepreneurial journey. I'm here for your success.

Acknowledgements

To my family, thank you for being there always. To my friends, my mentors, and my colleagues, thank you for the encouragement, the support, the laughter, and the good times. I truly appreciate and love you all.

About the Author

Blanche Greaux grew up, lived, went to school, worked, and started a business in the Caribbean. She has a Bachelor's degree in Communications from Temple University, and a Master's degree in Hospitality and Tourism Management from the University of Central Florida.

She currently lives in Orlando, Florida, and is also a licensed real estate agent in Florida. Her interests include reading, real estate investing, and mentoring. She is currently a mentor for the Branson Centre for Entrepreneurship Caribbean, and has served as both a mentor and advisory board member.

Notes

Notes

Notes

Notes

www.ingramcontent.com/pod-product-compliance
Ingram Content Group UK Ltd.
Pitfield, Milton Keynes, MK11 3LW, UK
UKHW061132310726
14090UKWH00035B/814

9 780578 737157